Images of Australia

Cathay Books

Preceding page

Sunset, near Quorn, South Australia.

Acknowledgments

Editorial: Blanche Hewitt
Design: Robert Moller
Photography: Weldon Trannies, Sydney
George Hall, p. 74

National Library of Australia
Cataloguing-in-Publication entry

Images of Australia

ISBN 0 947 334 00 9

1. Australia – Description and travel – 1976 –
— Views.

994.06'3

First published in Australia by Rigby Publishers 1985
This revised edition published in 1989 by
Octopus Publishing Group Australia Pty Ltd,
85 Abinger St, Richmond, Vic 3121
By arrangement with Weldon Russell Pty Ltd
A member of the Weldon International Group of Companies
Copyright © 1985, 1989 Weldon Russell Pty Ltd,
All rights reserved
Wholly designed and typeset in Australia
Produced by Mandarin Offset, Hong Kong

Contents

The edge of our
Island-Continent

Preceding page

Table Cape, near Wynyard, Tasmania.

Above

The coastline at Venus Bay, South Australia.

Right

Bay near Hazards Beach on the Freycinet Peninsula, Tasmania.

8

Above

Brampton Island off the coast of north-east
Queensland.

Right

Cape Leveque, north-west of Broome in Western
Australia.

10

Above

Shipwreck off Fraser Island.

The
Landscape

Preceding page

The Gordon River in Tasmania's south-west.

Right

A valley near Woodside in the Adelaide Hills, South Australia.

Preceding page

Old farmhouse, northern New South Wales.

Above

The border between Queensland and South Australia.

Right

Sunset near Quorn, South Australia.

Preceding page

Winter scene in the Grampians, Victoria.

Above

Old well in the Australian outback between
Birdsville and Cordillo Downs.

Right

Old farmhouse in the Warrumbungle Ranges of
New South Wales.

Above

Early morning mist over the Glenelg River at
Nelson in Victoria.

Right

Sand pattern made by crabs on the beach at Fraser
Island off the Queensland coast.

28

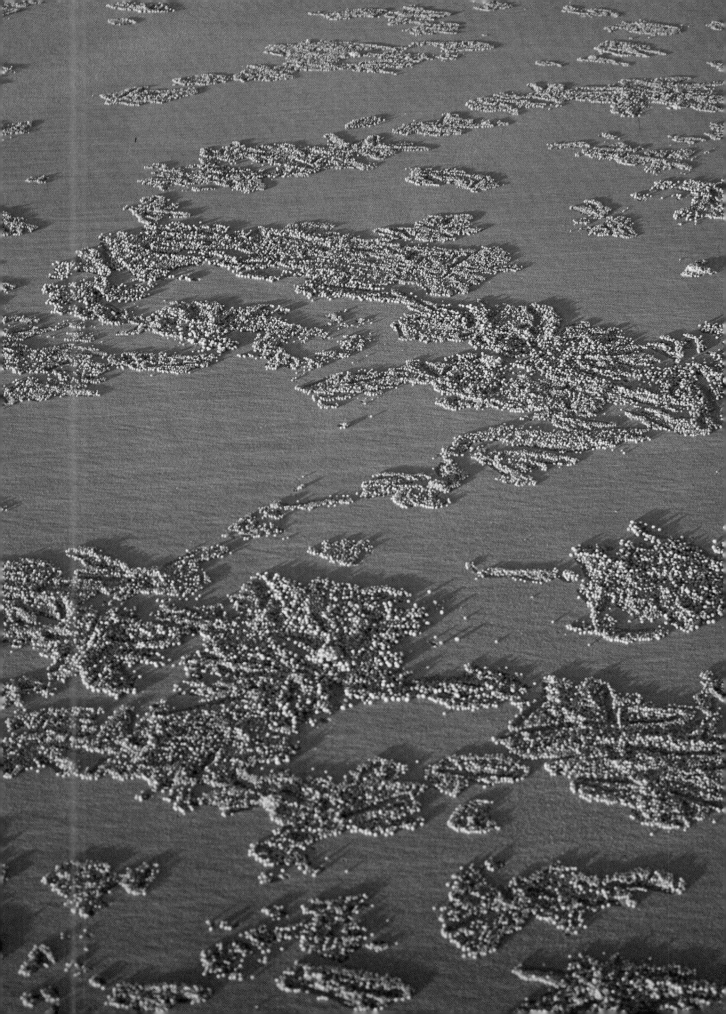

Preceding page

Abandoned homestead between Birdsville and
Cordillo Downs.

Above

Sunset at Ayers Rock, Aboriginal sacred site, in the
Northern Territory.

Right

Dust storm between Port Augusta and Port Pirie in
the mid-north of South Australia.

34

Above

Geikie Gorge in the Kimberley Ranges of Western Australia.

Above right

Sandstone erosion at Rainbow Gorge, Fraser Island.

Below right

Staked claims at Coober Pedy, South Australia.

Looking west from Table Cape, Tasmania.

Here Before Us

Preceding page

Cycads are found in the tropical and near-tropical zones of Australia. These examples are growing in the Northern Territory.

Above

Blackboy (*Kingia australis*) in the Kalbarri National Park, Western Australia.

Right

Baobab trees. Western Australia. The Australian Baobab tree grows on sandy plains and low stony ridges, from the Derby district in the Kimberleys to Arnhem Land, rarely ranging more than 160 kilometres inland.

Above

Staghorn fern. Fraser Island.

Right

Curtain fig tree. About sixty species of fig tree occur in Australia and, with the exception of four, all are found in Queensland.

42

Above

The Kangaroo Paw is the floral emblem of Western Australia and is native to that State.

Right

Sturt's Desert Pea. Named after the explorer, Charles Sturt, this brightly coloured, trailing plant flourishes in the sandy inland areas of Australia, flowering mainly in October, but sometimes in August, depending on the rainfall.

Preceding page

Pandanus favours swampy localities which are flooded during the wet season. This group of *Pandanus* is growing in a flood plain in the Northern Territory's Kakadu National Park.

Above

Golden Dryandra. Stirling Ranges, Western Australia. Native to Western Australia, the genus is named after the Swedish botanist, Jonas Dryander.

Right

Paperbark forest. Coastal Queensland.

48

Above

Pine trees on Fraser Island off the Queensland coast. The name 'pine' is given to a number of different indigenous conifers. *Pinus* (the true pine) occurs in the Australian region only as an introduction, being practically confined to the northern hemisphere.

Right

Pelicans on Lake Alexandrina, South Australia.

Right

Echidna (spiny anteater). Northern Territory.

The Blue-tongue lizard is harmless, but uses its
tongue in a threatening display when disturbed.

Right

The Kookaburra, a member of the kingfisher family
with a call resembling raucous human laughter.

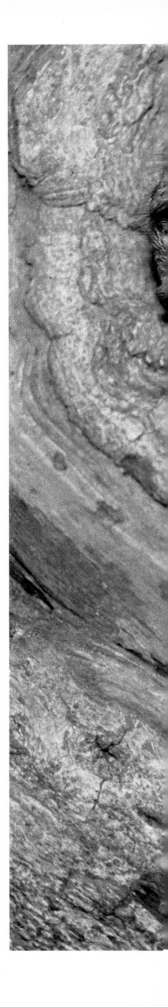

Above

Corellas in the Simpson Desert.

Right

The Tawny frogmouth is a noctural bird common throughout Australia.

56

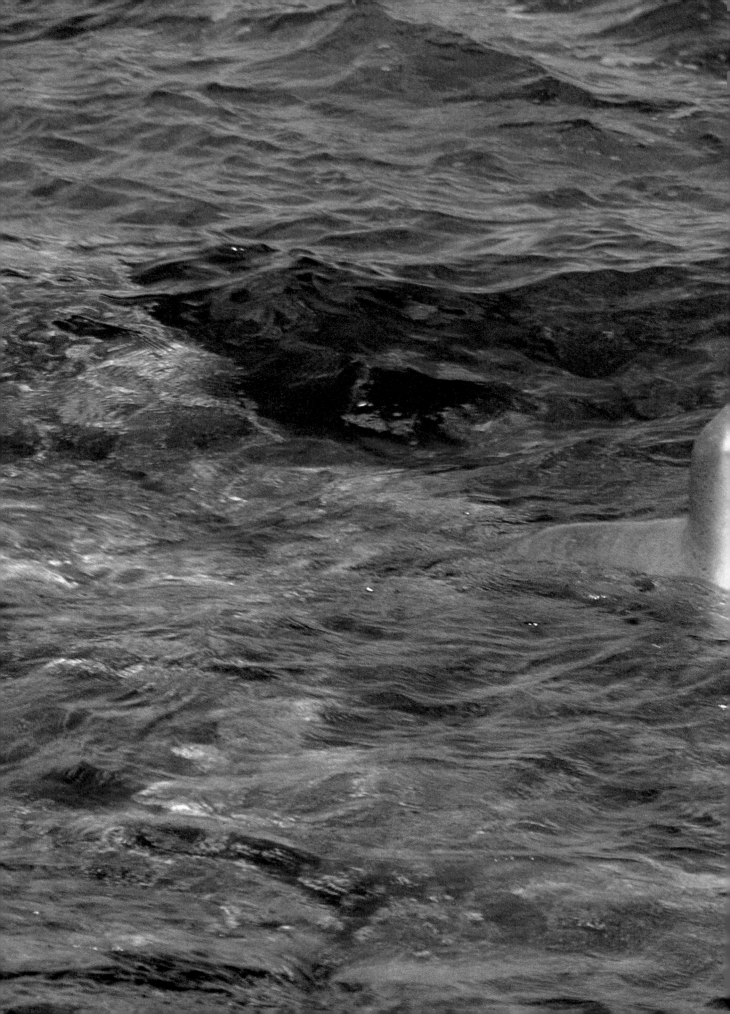

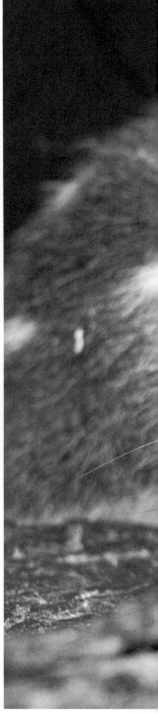

Preceding page

Sealions. Eyre Peninsula, South Australia.

Above

Brush-tailed possum (herbivorous, tree-dwelling marsupial). Northern Territory.

Right

Quoll (native cat). Northern Territory.

60

Above

Dingo (Australian wild dog). Northern Territory.

Above right

Euro (stocky, coarse-haired kangaroo). Gammon
Ranges, South Australia.

Right

Dragon lizard in the Gammon Ranges, South
Australia.

62

Hairy-nosed wombat. Eyre Peninsula, South
Australia.

The
Built Environment

Above

The Strand Arcade, Sydney (c. 1891) was designed
in the Edwardian Classical style and built of
stuccoed brick with a cast-iron roof structure. It
remains a fashionable shopping area.

Right

Aerial view of Adelaide, capital of South Australia.
In the foreground is the Adelaide Cricket Ground
with the River Torrens, the Festival Centre and the
commercial centre of the city behind.

Preceding page

The town of Clare, 140 kilometres from Adelaide, was settled in 1842 and named after County Clare in Ireland. It is the centre of a productive agricultural area and the Clare Valley is the home of some of South Australia's finest wines.

Above and Right

In 1915, opals were discovered at Coober Pedy in northern South Australia. This is now one of the richest sources of opal in the country. Coober Pedy is an Aboriginal name meaning 'white fellows' hole in the ground'. Many locals live in dugouts and caves to escape the extremes of temperature.

The Sydney Harbour Bridge, seen here in the evening light, links the North and South Shores of the city. It carries an eight-lane highway, two train-tracks, a cycle-way and a footpath.

Above right

Sydney's spectacular Opera House, riding majestically on Bennelong Point, gives tangible form to the adventurous spirit of a young nation, increasingly confident of its own cultural identity.

Below right

The corner of Pulteney Street and North Terrace, Adelaide, with Scots Church (1851) in the fore-ground.

Right

Bontharambo Homestead. Wangaratta, Victoria. A fine two-storeyed home of brick, stone and stucco, built in 1855, surrounded almost completely by a single-storey arcade and dominated by an eighteen-metre tower.

Right

The Cordillo Downs homestead (c. 1880) in the
north-eastern corner of South Australia has a semi-
circular roof, designed to economise on roof timbers
which were scarce in the area.

84

Preceding page

This old weatherboard farmhouse is situated on the Atherton Tablelands of north Queensland, a fertile region where dairying, timber-milling and the growing of tobacco and peanuts is the backbone of primary production.

Above right

The Goldmines Hotel, Bendigo, dates from 1857. It is one of the most architecturally important hotels in Bendigo, with a two-storey decorative cast-iron verandah and an elegant cement-rendered facade. The licence is still in the hands of the original family.

Below right

The Courthouse. Dubbo, New South Wales. Built in the Victorian Classical style between 1886 and 1890, it was designed in the office of the Colonial Architect, James Barnet. The exterior is dominated by a central portico with symmetrical wings. Inside, the court room retains the original fittings.

Sydney University. In 1854, the Colonial Architect, Edmund Blacket resigned his post to devote his attention to the design of the University buildings. His stated inspiration was the quadrangular precincts of Oxford and Cambridge. The foundation stone was laid in 1855.

Right

The burnt-out shell of the Eagle-on-the-Hill Hotel at Crafers in the Adelaide Hills, destroyed in the Ash Wednesday bushfire, 1983 and subsequently rebuilt.

Ruins of the penal settlement at Port Macquarie on
the north coast of New South Wales.

The
People

Preceding page

Grader driver on an isolated stretch of the Birdsville
Track.

Above

A Santos gas pipeline worker.

Right

Bookmakers at the Oakbank Races.

Above

Race-goers at Oakbank, South Australia.

Above right

News stand in Sydney's Martin Place.

Below right

Outback race meeting at Timber Creek in the
Northern Territory.

96

Above

Fencemakers' camp at Alton Downs.

Right

'Old George', dingo hunter by trade, photographed near Alton Downs in the Australian outback.

98

Above

Spectators at the Broome rodeo, Western Australia.

Right

Schoolchildren in the South Australian outback between Andamooka and Roxby Downs.

Far right

Local resident outside his cottage at Streaky Bay on South Australia's Eyre Peninsula.

104

Australian test cricketer, Dennis Lillee with young
fans at the Adelaide Oval, South Australia.

The
Good Earth

110

A bountiful harvest from the vineyards of the
Sevenhill Monastery, Clare, South Australia, where
the Jesuits have been producing wine for over a
century.

The
Depths Beneath

Above

Gas pipeline worker in the outback of South Australia.

Right

Steelworker at the BHP (Broken Hill Proprietary Ltd.) Steelworks, Whyalla, South Australia.

116

Gas and oil drilling rig. Cooper Basin, South
Australia.